MW01144328

Seeds of a Nation

Washington

Stuart A. Kallen

**KIDHAVEN
PRESS**™

THOMSON

GALE™

San Diego • Detroit • New York • San Francisco • Cleveland
New Haven, Conn. • Waterville, Maine • London • Munich

LIBRARY OF CONGRESS CATALOGING-IN-PUBLICATION DATA

Kallen, Stuart A., 1955–
  Washington / by Stuart A. Kallen.
    p. cm. — (Seeds of a nation)
Includes bibliographical references and index.
Summary: Discusses the history of Washington state, from the lives of the Native Americans who were there before the European settlers came, through the arrival of the railroad, up to its statehood in 1889.
  ISBN 0-7377-1480-8 (alk. paper)
  1. Washington (State)—History—To 1889—Juvenile literature. [1. Washington (State)—History—To 1889.] I. Title. II. Series.
  F891 .K35 2003
  979.7—dc21
                                                              2002015472

Printed in the United States of America

Contents

Chapter One

The Native Americans

Washington is a state known for its awe-inspiring natural wonders such as a rugged Pacific coastline, mossy green rain forests, and glacier-capped mountains. The state is home to nearly 6 million people and is located in the northwest corner of the United States between Oregon,

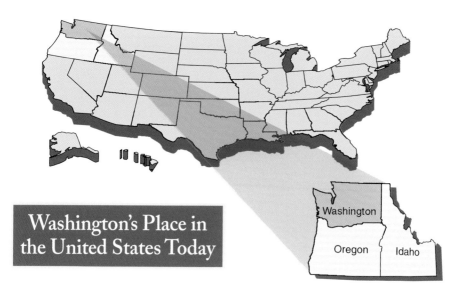

Washington's Place in the United States Today

Washington

Oregon   Idaho

Makah Indians carved canoes from wood. They look much like this model.

Canada, the Pacific Ocean, and Idaho. Washington's largest city, Seattle, has been called one of the most livable cities in America and is famous for its high-tech and trade industries. But long before Washington took its place as the fifteenth most populous state in America, it was inhabited by dozens of Native American tribes whose lives and cultures were as rich and varied as the natural scenery.

Totems and Whales

The Makah Indians made their home on the northwestern tip of the Olympic Peninsula for more than ten thousand years. Up to one hundred inches of rain falls on this region every year. The Makah homeland was surrounded by a dense forest of towering Douglas fir, cedar, spruce, and hemlock. The wood from trees was used by skilled carvers to make canoes, tools, and dishes. The bark and needles were used for clothing.

Faces and mythical creatures decorate this brightly colored totem pole.

The Makah also used the wood to construct huge one-room wooden structures called **longhouses,** where more than one hundred people lived together. The outer walls of the longhouses were decorated with fantastic paintings of **supernatural** animals from traditional Native American stories.

Each longhouse was marked by a towering **totem pole** up to fifty feet tall. These totems were decorated with human faces and fierce-looking mythical creatures. Their images told stories of respected chiefs, great deeds, and spiritual events. Similar figures resembling eagles, ravens, beavers, wolves, and other animals were also carved into wooden masks and hats.

The Makah ate fish, clams, mussels, and wild fruit such as blackberries, huckleberries, and salmonberries. Their most prized food, however, came from whales. During whale hunts, the Makah set out in eight-man cedar canoes to battle twenty-ton gray whales, sperm whales, and humpbacks. The men were armed with only long harpoons tipped with sharpened mussel shells and a barbed point of elk bone.

As in many other aspects of Indian life, the whale hunt had deep spiritual meaning. Before the hunt Makah whalers cleaned their bodies, painted their faces, fasted, and performed religious rituals. Men did not speak of the coming hunt because they believed that the whales could hear them and might stay away. Once a whale was killed, the Makah thanked the animal for its sacrifice and continued to honor its soul in death.

The Sacred Salmon

South of the Makah homeland, the Chinook tribes also lived in longhouse villages on the Pacific coast. The Chinook survived on a wide variety of fish including herring, smelt, cod, trout, and halibut. Salmon, however, was the most important fish. And like the Makah, the Chinook had important legends concerning their main source of food. The Chinook believed that salmon were supernatural creatures that looked like human beings and lived in fantastic houses beneath the ocean waves. The Chinook also believed that every spring, the humanlike salmon would take on the appearance of fish and return from the sea to swim upstream and lay eggs.

During the salmon's swim upstream, the tribes speared the fish with harpoons or simply scooped the creatures out of the water with baskets. The Native Americans believed that the fish had given their bodies, but not their souls, for the well being of the tribe. After the fish were eaten the bones were returned to the sea, where it was believed they would become human again and repeat the cycle.

Every spring the rivers of Washington flashed silver and pink with millions of **spawning** salmon. These fish were so plentiful, in fact, that the tribes could not possibly eat all they caught. The extra fish were dried and smoked and loaded into canoes. The Chinook then pad-

The salmon provided a rich source of food for the Chinook Indians and were also used for trade throughout the Washington region.

The Native Americans

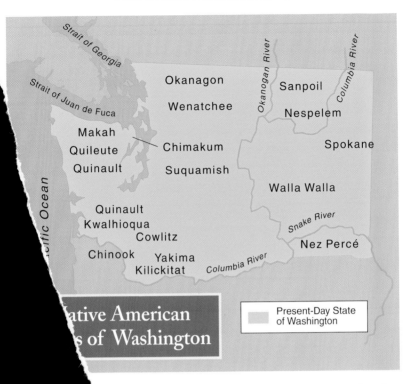

Strait of Georgia

Strait of Juan de Fuca

Pacific Ocean

Okanogan River

Columbia River

Okanagon

Wenatchee

Sanpoil

Nespelem

Makah

Quileute

Quinault

Chimakum

Suquamish

Spokane

Quinault

Kwalhioqua

Cowlitz

Walla Walla

Snake River

Chinook   Yakima

Kilickitat   Columbia River

Nez Percé

ative American
s of Washington

Present-Day State
of Washington

Columbia River every summer to trade the
s that lived inland.

st traders on the Columbia, the Chinook
seashells, and other goods from the
buffalo skins, and tobacco. During
the Chinook met other Indians,
hundreds of miles, from as far
nd the Great Plains.

h

ained in trade, the
s with family and
ticed at a ceremony
eans "giving" in the
tlatch was held, a host

would invite guests to his home and give each person a gift. Those of high rank received the most valued gifts. In return the guest was expected to give a gift of equal value to the host.

Potlatches were held following important events such as weddings, births, deaths, or coming-of-age cere monies. The events were so important that the hos sometimes spent months, or even years, gathering t necessary blankets, jewelry, statues, masks, hats, and f needed for the hundreds of invited guests. In additi gift giving, potlatches featured special costumes, da singing, feasting, and religious rituals.

The Plateau Tribes

While the Chinook led comfortable lives in villages along the coast, east of the Cascade other Native American tribes lived in an e ent way. Like the coastal tribes, the lives Walla Walla, Nez Percé, and Cayuse natural features that dominated th these tribes in central and eastern region dominated by sunny s than ocean and forest.

The only building treeless plains, kno were mud, grasses, The plateau tribes u called earth lodges. holes, thirty feet in dia of mud, grass, and will

Pac...

N...
Tribe...

dled up the ...
fish with tribe...

As the greate...
bartered salmon, ...
coast for stone tools, ...
these trade missions, ...
some of whom had walked ...
away as the Rocky Mounta...

Exchanging Gifts at t...

With a plentiful supply o...
Chinook valued excha...
friends. This generosit...
known as a potlatch, ...
Chinook language. W...

n
-
ts
he
ood
on to
ncing,

permanent
Mountains
entirely differ-
of the Yakima,
were ruled by the
their homeland. But
Washington lived in a
kies and grasslands rather

als available on the nearly
Columbia River **plateau**,
that grew near riverbeds.
materials to build homes
simply three-foot-deep
ered with a domed roof
es. From four to eight

families lived in each lodge. The clever design of these structures protected the families from searing heat, pouring rain, bone-chilling winds, and freezing snow.

In the late spring, the Yakima and other tribes left their earth-lodge villages and set up camps along the upper Columbia River. The tribes spent the summer gathering wild food and herbs, fishing, and hunting elk, deer, bighorn sheep, and birds.

With plenty of food, life was easy and the season was spent feasting, dancing, trading, and performing religious ceremonies. In addition, tribe members liked to have fun by running footraces, wrestling, and gambling.

The plateau tribes built earth lodges out of mud, grass, and tree branches.

Teams of up to twenty Yakima women played a game known as shinny. The object of the game was to drive deerskin balls into the opposing team's goal. The balls were kicked and hit with feet and sticks. This popular game was often played for hours every day.

In the 1700s the Yakima way of life changed when Europeans brought horses to the region. The Yakima quickly became skilled riders and began traveling east to the Great Plains to hunt bison. Soon after, American explorers arrived by the dozens in Washington, forever altering the traditional ways of the Yakima, Chinook, Makah, and other tribes in the region.

Chapter Two

Explorers and Traders

I n the late sixteenth century European ships sailed into view along the Washington coast. The first of these ships was piloted in 1592 by Spanish sea captain Juan de Fuca. He glided into the narrow body of water, or **strait**, that now bears his name. Over the course of the next two centuries, the Spanish continued exploring the region, naming places such as the San Juan Islands in Puget Sound. But the men on these ships never went ashore, and their passing had little impact on the native populations.

It was not until the eighteenth century that the first European set foot in Washington. In 1775 two Spanish ships commanded by Bruno de Heceta and Juan Francisco de Bodega y Quadra were on their way from Mexico to Alaska when they sent a landing party ashore near present-day Point Grenville on the Olympic Peninsula. As the crewmen filled barrels with fresh drinking water from the Hoh River, a group of Native Americans seized

Washington's rugged and jagged coastline made landing and exploring a difficult task.

their small landing craft. A fight ensued and the Spaniards were killed. Heceta then turned his ship around and headed back to Mexico. Quadra went to Alaska before returning home.

Early British Traders

Four years later a ship carrying British landing crew landed along the Washington coast. These men broughts gifts and were treated well by the Native Americans. The crew noticed that several tribe members were wearing beautiful robes made from otter fur. The natives, who had no metal tools, were willing to trade their robes for British knives, nails, and even useless scraps of iron.

After acquiring several dozen robes, the British sailed to China, where they sold the garments for a huge sum of money. When they returned home, they told others about the fine furs traded by the Indians. Within a few years, dozens of British traders arrived in Washington.

Native Americans of the Pacific Northwest trapped furs for trade with the English.

At that time relations between Europeans and Native Americans were peaceful because both benefitted from the exchange of goods. British explorers were by then bringing better-quality goods such as axes, metal-tipped harpoons, iron cookware, and other items to trade. These items were highly prized because they allowed the Indians to perform time-consuming tasks with much less work. For example, a man using an iron ax could cut

British explorer Captain George Vancouver's ship HMS Discovery *ended up on the rocks in Queen Charlotte's Sound, in what would become British Columbia. Curious Native Americans paddled out to witness the end of the ship.*

down a tree in one-tenth the time as a man using a stone ax. And because otters were plentiful, natives were willing to trade dozens of furs for a single iron tool.

As the traditional traders in the region, the Chinook carried the items they received from the British to trade with the inland tribes. Before long, in many tribes European iron goods had replaced traditional tools previously made from bone, stone, wood, and shell.

Unfortunately, the Europeans brought more than iron. They also imported devastating diseases such as smallpox, measles, and cholera to the tribes. The native populations had no **immunity** to these illnesses, and thousands quickly died.

Vancouver's Adventure

Despite the negative affect on the tribes, the rich fur trade continued to attract British explorers to Washington. In 1792 Captain George Vancouver sailed his ship *Discovery* through the Strait of Juan de Fuca, where he discovered the great body of water east of the Olympic Peninsula. Vancouver named the inlet Puget Sound after his lieutenant Peter Puget.

The water in the **sound** was too shallow for Vancouver's 330-ton ship, so a crew paddled out in several small rowboats. These boats, each rowed by five pairs of men, were weighed down with muskets, pistols, trade goods, tents, navigating equipment, survey equipment, food, and wine. Like other crews at the time, the men in the crew were young, most of them between the ages of thirteen and twenty.

As the team explored and mapped Puget Sound, they were shadowed on land by wary Native Americans who watched their every move. Finally, the crew was confronted by a group of Salish Indian warriors, who were angry that the intruders had taken game and fish without permission from their honored hunting grounds. The frightened Captain Vancouver ordered a cannon to be shot across the water, and the natives quickly recognized the power of the Europeans' guns. Instead of war, the two groups of men from far different cultures began a friendly exchange of goods to ease the tension. By sunset the trading had reached such a fevered pitch that the warriors began to undress, offering their clothes for barter.

After this exchange, the men returned to *Discovery*, having been the first Europeans to map Puget Sound. Along the way, Vancouver claimed the entire region for England and gave names to many features he had seen including Whidbey Island and the distant Mount Baker and Mount Rainier.

Walking to Washington

Explorers continued to travel to Washington by sea. But in the early nineteenth century, a team of famous explorers were the first white men to travel by land to the region.

In 1803 the United States bought all of the land between the Mississippi River and the Pacific Ocean from France as part of the Louisiana Purchase. To explore the region, President Thomas Jefferson appointed his private secretary, Meriwether Lewis, to head an **expedition** across the Rocky Mountains to the Pacific

Sacagawea (center) helps Lewis and Clark find their way to the Pacific Northwest.

Northwest. Lewis invited William Clark to join him, and the pair recruited forty-six men to accompany them on their journey. This team had artists, mapmakers, biologists, and other scientists to study and record plants, animals, minerals, and scenery along the way.

The Lewis and Clark expedition headed west from St. Louis, Missouri, in May 1804, traveling by canoe, on foot, and on horseback. After a grueling journey across the Rocky Mountains, the men finally paddled down the Columbia River and reached the Pacific Ocean in November 1805. By then the damp, cold northwestern rains had begun and the expedition spent a miserable winter camped on the southern banks of the Columbia River in present-day Oregon. The men finally returned to St. Louis in September 1806.

The Lewis and Clark expedition was a complete success. Scientists who traveled with the team recorded volumes of information about the continent, proving that America was rich with lumber, minerals, and fur-bearing animals.

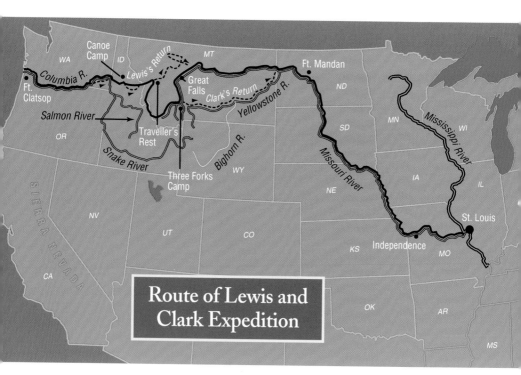

Route of Lewis and Clark Expedition

When news of the Lewis and Clark expedition was printed in newspapers, hundreds of fur trappers, settlers, and explorers set out on foot to the lands that include present-day Washington, Oregon, and Idaho. Along the way, they faced many hardships. But those who succeeded found a land where nature rewarded their efforts with a bounty of riches.

Chapter Three

The Settlers

The first settlers in what became the state of Washington were Canadian, British, and American trappers who moved there in the early nineteenth century to work in the fur trade. They were inspired by reports from the Lewis and Clark expedition. These reports stated that Washington was inhabited by millions of beaver and other fur-bearing animals.

In the early 1800s the pelts of these creatures were as valuable as gold. No proper gentleman would appear in public without a beaver hat perched on his head. And rich, fashionable women prized clothing with fur collars, cuffs, and other decorations. Fur trappers could barely keep up with the demand for pelts from fox, otter, panther, bear, deer, and especially beaver. These American furs were also in demand in England, France, and other European countries. Fur-trading companies exported the pelts of more than 1 million animals every year.

By filling this demand, fur-trading companies were some of the wealthiest businesses in the world. The largest of these companies was the British-owned Hudson's Bay Company which, by 1800, had been buying and selling furs from North America for 130 years. This giant, based in Canada, was challenged in 1784 by another Canadian business, the North West Company, formed by independent fur traders.

Astor's Dream

Canada was not the only country that had fur-trading companies. John Jacob Astor, a wealthy American fur trader, founded the Pacific Fur Company in 1810. Astor had a dream of establishing a series of trading

Trappers in the Pacific Northwest harvest beaver pelts for trade.

posts along the Columbia River. Beaver pelts would be purchased from trappers and Native Americans at each post, collected at a fort along the Pacific coast, and shipped to China at a huge profit. In addition to furs,

American trader John Jacob Astor founded the Pacific Fur Company in 1810.

settlers working for Astor would grow food and sell it to Russia, while loggers cut down and sold trees for sale in Asia.

In 1811, Astor sent out two expeditions of men, known as Astorians, to carry out his vision in Washington. The first settlers arrived by ship in July, setting up camp on the Oregon side of the Columbia River. There, the Astorians constructed four log huts they grandly called Fort Astoria in honor of their boss.

The second expedition set out to travel by land from St. Louis, following the route established by Lewis and Clark. Three months later this eight-man expedition, led by David Stuart, settled on a strip of sand on the Okanogan River, where it flowed into the Columbia River in central Washington. There they built a little trading post out of driftwood and called it Fort Okanogan.

First American Settlement

When the fort was finished, it was the northernmost outpost of Astor's fur empire—and the first American settlement in Washington. This post was on a well-established Native American trading route where tribes had traditionally gathered to trap beaver, catch fish, trade goods, and hold potlatches.

In September Stuart's expedition left Fort Okanogan to sail down the Columbia River to Fort Astoria. Stuart left behind one man, Alexander Ross, to spend the winter trading with the local tribes. Ross was a shrewd trader and

Beaver pelts hang in a replica of a nineteenth-century fur trading room.

obtained pelts worth $10,000 for merchandise valued at only $160.

While Fort Okanogan was turning a profit, traders at Fort Astoria were facing stiff competition from the North West Company. In 1812 traders at the fort sold Astoria to the North West Company at a huge loss to Astor. Two years later the fort was seized by the British navy and renamed Fort George.

Life at Fort Vancouver

In 1821 Hudson's Bay Company bought out the North West Company. With total control over the Washington fur trade, the company established its headquarters in the heart of fur country along the Columbia River. Fort Vancouver, as it was called, was named after the eighteenth-century explorer George Vancouver. Although there were about a dozen other trading posts in Washington, Fort Vancouver quickly became the most important.

Fort Vancouver was the most important trading post in Washington.

Hudson's Bay Company hired John McLoughlin to run the operations at Fort Vancouver. McLoughlin believed in dealing fairly with the local Native American tribes but restricted trade items to blankets, pots and pans, buttons, cloth, and tools. Hoping to maintain a peaceful environment, McLoughlin allowed the sale of only limited amounts of ammunition for their firearms.

In addition to managing the trading, McLoughlin directed the settlers to plant more than two thousand acres of peas, barley, corn, buckwheat, wheat, oats, and potatoes. Workers also planted the first apple and pear orchards in the West. In addition, the settlers raised cows, pigs, sheep, and chickens to feed the fort's growing population.

McLoughlin was interested in more than trading. He wanted to establish a British-style village in the Washington wilderness. He ordered the construction of fine homes along with a church, a school, a library, and even a theater. Mills were set up to grind grain into flour, a smokehouse produced dried salmon, and a distillery made beer and whiskey. The fort's sawmill produced finished lumber that craftsmen turned into fine furniture.

Trapper's Life

Fort Vancouver was a small civilization in the wilderness. But the trappers who worked for the company led a difficult life in a dangerous environment. Trapping was done mostly in the cold, wet months of late fall and early spring when animal fur was thickest. In the summer, before the season began, trappers spent their time around

A trapper astride his wading horse waits patiently for beavers.

Fort Vancouver collecting snowshoes, tents, clothing, blankets, dried food, ammunition, new traps, and other supplies.

To capture beaver, trappers worked all day in freezing rivers, setting traps underwater to catch the water-loving animals. After several months of this backbreaking labor, the trapper might come back to the fort with three hundred to four hundred pelts. These could be sold for several thousand dollars. This was a huge sum at a time when a skilled carpenter made about $1.50 a day. Every year, however, several trappers failed to return. Some died in the woods from accidents, starvation, or disease. Others may have been murdered over disputes with Native Americans or other trappers.

After selling the pelts, trappers took off a month or more to rest and relax. Groups of these men held gatherings at campsites, where hundreds of trappers spent their days drinking, gambling, and fighting.

While trappers struggled in the wilderness, events across the ocean were about to change their way of life. Beaver top hats, which had been popular for several hundred years, fell out of fashion in Europe. And even as this occurred, the number of beavers and other animals had declined rapidly in Washington. All those years of unlimited trapping had pushed beavers to the edge of extinction. Trade fell off, and by the 1850s farming had replaced trapping as the main occupation in Washington. Fort Vancouver, along with most of the trading posts in the Oregon Country, had become ghost towns.

Chapter Four

From Territory to State

In the early 1800s fur traders from the United States, Canada, and Great Britain worked together in the Oregon Country. But both the American and British governments laid claim to the land, and disputes over ownership were often heated. Americans wanted the land to be part of the continental United States. The British, who ruled Canada, wanted to make Washington part of that country.

By the 1830s the British navy controlled the Washington coast, and the British-owned Hudson's Bay Company dominated the fur trade. But American officials insisted that the United States had a claim on the area because Lewis and Clark were the first to explore Washington's interior. Americans also believed that John Jacob Astor had established rights to the area when he built Fort Astoria and a string of other trading posts across the region in the 1810s.

Oregon Fever

Tensions grew between the United States and Great Britain in the early 1840s, when thousands of Americans walked the Oregon Trail from Independence, Missouri, to Washington. These excited people had heard that free farmland was available in Washington. Their rush to move there was known as Oregon Fever. Meanwhile, Britain grew increasingly alarmed as the trickle of American pioneers turned into a flood.

In the rush known as Oregon Fever, Americans seeking free farmland reach Washington.

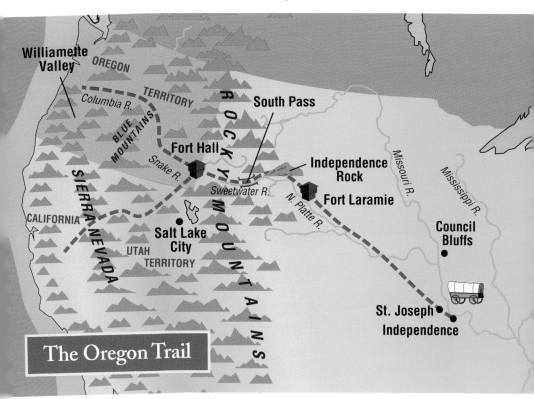

The Oregon Trail

The British let the new arrivals live in peace, but many Americans began calling for war. These people demanded that Great Britain give up the entire Oregon Country—Washington, Oregon, and Idaho—to the United States.

When James K. Polk was elected president in 1844, he began negotiations with Great Britain to obtain the Oregon Country for the United States. The British were having their own social unrest as well as a conflict in Ireland. As a result, Britain decided not to enter into war with the United States. In 1846 President Polk met with British authorities and signed the Oregon Treaty, establishing the U.S. border with Canada where it still stands today.

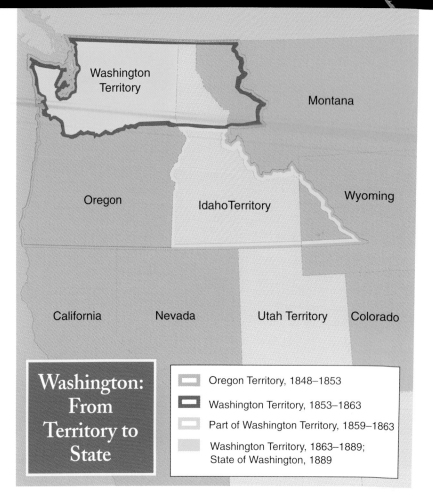

Washington Territory

Montana

Oregon

IdahoTerritory

Wyoming

California   Nevada   Utah Territory   Colorado

Washington: From Territory to State

Oregon Territory, 1848–1853

Washington Territory, 1853–1863

Part of Washington Territory, 1859–1863

Washington Territory, 1863–1889; State of Washington, 1889

The Changing Shape of Washington

In 1848 the U.S. Congress created the Oregon Territory out of present-day Wyoming, Montana, Idaho, Oregon, and Washington. Oregon City was named capital of the territory. Oregon had a much larger population than Washington, but settlers in the northern part of the territory felt the new capital was too far away to serve their needs.

In 1851 the *Columbian* newspaper in Olympia initiated a campaign to convince Congress to make Washington a separate territory. Two years later, on March 2, 1853, Congress granted the request and established the Washington Territory, naming it in honor of the first U.S.

president. Olympia was selected as capital of the territory and Isaac Ingalls Stevens was appointed governor.

The new territory was much larger than the state is today. The southern border with Oregon along the Columbia River has not changed, but to the west the territory included the Idaho panhandle and parts of western Montana. This huge area contained few settlers, however. Government figures showed only 1,050 settlers living in the Washington Territory.

The shape of the Washington Territory changed in 1859 when Oregon became the thirty-third state. At that time, parts of the former Oregon Territory—all of Idaho and northwest Wyoming—were added to the Washington Territory.

In 1863, Congress moved the borders once again, cropping off Idaho and Wyoming. This move finally left the territory with the current boundaries of Washington state.

Obtaining Indian Lands

Even as territory borders shifted, Washington's population continued to grow. And the newcomers were different from earlier pioneers. The fur trappers had been content to settle around a few scattered forts, but the new arrivals wanted large areas of land for farming. The Native Americans viewed this trend with worry and fear, but there was little they could do to fight the growing power of the United States.

Furthermore, Governor Stevens was eager to obtain Indian lands. Almost as soon as he became governor,

Stevens began signing treaties with the coastal tribes. They agreed to give up their lands for small sums of money. They also agreed to move to reservations, where they would be allowed to hunt and fish in their traditional manner. These tribes depended on fish and seafood, and they were able to survive under the conditions of the new treaties because they did not need much land to obtain their food.

Although the coastal tribes peacefully sold off their territory, they did so with great sadness. Their pain was expressed in a moving speech given in 1854 by Chief Seattle, leader of the Suquamish people:

Native Americans hunt and fish along coastal Washington.

Chief Seattle of the Suquamish tribe mourned the coastal tribes' loss of land rights.

There was a time when our people covered the whole land as the waves of a wind-ruffled sea cover its shell-paved floor. But that time has long since passed away with the greatness of tribes now almost forgotten. . . . Your God loves your people and hates mine; he has forsaken his red children; he makes your people wax strong every day, and soon they will fill the land; while our people are ebbing away like a fast-receding tide.

The Yakima Wars

Tribes in eastern Washington were also pressured to sign away their land rights. These tribes on the Columbia River plateau, such as the Yakima, were used to traveling long distances on horseback and required huge tracts of land to survive. Governor Stevens ignored this as he drew up plans to sell vast sections of tribal homeland to white farmers. Meanwhile, a U.S. Army expedition was sent to survey the lands for building roads and railroads through the heart of the Yakima homeland.

Stevens called a council near Walla Walla in 1855, and more than five thousand Native Americans attended the meeting. Members of the Yakima, Walla Walla, Cayuse, and Nez Percé tribes signed treaties giving up more than seventeen thousand square miles of land to the United States in return for $200,000. In addition, the Native Americans were given large reservations to live on.

Almost as soon as the treaties were signed, gold was discovered near present-day Colville, on the reservation promised to the Yakima. As hundreds of gold seekers poured onto the Yakima land, fights broke out between the Native Americans and the intruders. Before long, the U.S. Army was sent in to fight the Yakima and defend the gold hunters. The war raged for several years, but the tribes were finally defeated in 1859.

Washington Becomes a State

With the war over, settlers began streaming into the Washington Territory. In the east, cattle ranchers and farmers were bringing thousands of cows and sheep to graze on the wide-open plains. In the west, the city of Seattle, named after the Suquamish chief, was growing rapidly. Meanwhile, thousands of miles of Indian trails were being developed into **stagecoach** roads. Still, the Washington Territory remained isolated from the rest of the United States because the territory was separated by dense forests and tall mountains. This changed dramatically in 1887 when the Northern Pacific Railroad was

A survey party poses next to the Northern Pacific Railroad. The railroad connected Washington to the rest of the United States.

completed. It linked Washington to the rest of the nation. The railroad allowed visitors to reach Washington in a matter of days, instead of months.

The railroad had a dramatic effect on Washington. While the population was little more than 75,000 in 1880, by 1889, 350,000 people lived in the state. On November 11, 1889, Washington became the forty-second state. Although it had taken more than thirty-five years to move from territory to state, the people of the Pacific coast, Olympic rain forests, Cascade Mountains, and broad eastern plains were proud citizens of the United States of America. Their state continued to grow until it became one of the most desirable places in the entire nation to live.

Facts About Washington

Population: 5,894,121

State capital: Olympia

Largest city: Seattle

State motto: Al-Ki (Native American word meaning "By and by")

State song: "Washington, My Home"

State nicknames: Evergreen State, Chinook State

State flower: coast rhododendron

State insect: green darner dragonfly

State tree: western hemlock

State animal: cougar

State bird: willow goldfinch

State fish: steelhead

State fossil: Columbian mammoth

State mineral: petrified wood

Glossary

expedition: A journey taken by a group of people to achieve a specific goal.

immunity: Resistance to a disease.

longhouses: Long, communal dwellings built of wood and bark where dozens of Native American families lived in separate small, open apartments.

plateau: An elevated, level expanse of land, so flat it is sometimes called tableland.

sound: A long, wide inlet such as a bay or a cove leading inland from an ocean.

spawning: The process of a fish laying eggs in order to reproduce.

stagecoach: A horse-drawn vehicle.

strait: A long, narrow channel joining two bodies of water.

supernatural: Referring to a deity or a magical god or goddess that exists beyond the natural world.

totem pole: A wood pillar painted with symbols.

For Further Exploration

Jeanne Oyawin Elder, *The Makah*. Austin, TX: Raintree, 2000. The history of the Native American tribe that makes its home on the northwestern tip of the Olympic Peninsula.

Ron Hirschi, *People of the Salmon and Cedar*. New York: Cobblehill Books, 1996. The history and culture of the Native American tribes of the Pacific Northwest.

Diane Hoyt-Goldsmith, *Totem Pole*. New York: Holiday House, 1990. A young boy describes how his father carved a totem pole for the Klallam tribe.

Sandy E. Powell, *Washington*. Minneapolis: Lerner Publications, 2002. An exploration of America's forty-second state from its Native American past to the twenty-first century.

Rebecca Stefoff, *Lewis and Clark*. New York: Chelsea Juniors, 1992. A biography of the two men who led the thirty-month expedition to the mouth of the Columbia River.

Index

Picture Credits

About the Author

Stuart A. Kallen is the author of more than 150 nonfiction books for children and young adults. He has written on topics ranging from the theory of relativity to the history of rock and roll. In addition, Kallen has written award-winning children's videos and television scripts. In his spare time, Kallen is a singer/songwriter/guitarist in San Diego, California.